SPIRITUAL DEPRESSION

A Lifting up for the Downcast

AUDU SUYUM

Copyright © 2016. All rights reserved.

No part of this publication may be reproduced, stored in a retrieval system or transmitted in any way by any means, electronic, mechanical, photocopy, recording or otherwise, without the prior permission of the author except as provided by USA copyright law.

The opinions expressed by the author are not necessarily those of Revival Waves of Glory Books & Publishing.

Published by Revival Waves of Glory Books & Publishing

PO Box 596 I Litchfield, Illinois 62056 USA

www.revivalwavesofgloryministries.com

Revival Waves of Glory Books & Publishing is committed to excellence in the publishing industry.

Book design Copyright © 2016 by Revival Waves of Glory Books & Publishing. All rights reserved.

Published in the United States of America

Paperback: 978-1-68411-182-4

Contents

Contents 3
PREFACE 4
INTRODUCTION 6
The Text 12
WORSHIP 13
ADOPTION 14
Immanence of God 14
Adoption: A Cry for Worship 17
ADORATION 21
Transcendence of God 21
HOLINESS 24
SUPPLICATION 29
REVIVAL 30
SURVIVAL 36
CONFESSION 39
DELIVERANCE 44
Notes 48

PREFACE

The idea of this book originated from the many mechanistic books on prayer, a scientific view and approach and the popular expression that prayer is as simple as dialing your friend's number for communication - all of which tend to make prayer- Christian prayer mechanical, too simple and pluralistic. Pluralistic in the sense that it cannot easily be differentiated from the religious and professional prayer of the other religious groups of the world.

My purpose therefore is to explain and establish the theological meaning and approach to prayer over and against the scientific view and approach to prayer by expounding the Lord's Prayer.

Prayer, I believe, let me assert, according to the Lord's Prayer, is both **worship** and **supplication**. It is worship because it emphasis redemption relationship first and it is supplication because it concerns and emphasis spiritual and physical needs.

With this understanding therefore we divided this booklet into two parts. Part one discusses prayer as worship whereas part two, prayer as supplication. My usage should

THE LORD'S PRAYER

not be taken loosely or figuratively. I used it to mean that prayer is worship and supplication as already asserted above.

INTRODUCTION

It's not an exaggeration to say that the Lord's Prayer is specially honored in the whole history of Christianity and spirituality in particular. It's honored in the church liturgy, in the sacraments and in the devotional life (private prayer). Today is the same practice. That tells how significant and necessary the prayer is.

But the question is: what is the Lord's Prayer? What is the reason and purpose of it? What has it got to teach us about prayer?

Questions like these are theological, and for a long time, theology, for the common person, has plagued the church. For the history of theology is a history of arguments, disputes, controversies and divisions. Because of this, the church, the modern church is no longer interested in theology and theological matters. Theology is dangerous – a merciless enemy of the truth and church. Theologians are skeptic professors, not true Christians. What the church needs is not "what-is" a book, but "how-to" a book. She needs some basic principles on how to make heaven, live her life and pray to God. But we should be aware of this detrimental and pernicious attitude. It's an apostate attitude. "The fool says there is no God" (Psalm 14). A fool is not primarily an atheist, but a person who hates knowledge (Prov. 1:7), knowledge of God – theology, one who is anti-theology, not interested in theology and theological questions.

Theology and theological questions are indispensable for the church. Christian faith, ministry and service are theology. To reject or belittle theology and its questions is to renounce God and faith. The sign of a declined Christianity is her little interest in theology and theological issues. The history of genuine Christianity is history of theology.

The result? Reformed, Protestant, Puritan and Evangelical Christianity. Christianity is theology and theological quest.

Prayer is theology. The Lord's Prayer is theological, and was given for theological reflection. But let's first, in general order, observe some propositional truths about the Lord's Prayer in reference to the above questions.

First, the Lord's Prayer is not a prayer *per se*. In other words, it's not a prayer in itself. It's a traditional error therefore, to go about reciting the prayer as some special kind of prayer. Indeed, it's mistaken to close your eyes to say the Lord's Prayer. Some women believers go to an extreme to display some signs of homage as to squatting down after saying the Amen. We may as well think of the Apostle Creed as some special prayer or confession in itself.

Nowhere in the Bible were the apostles and the believers in general found to recite the Lord's Prayer in private or co-operate worship. It's not surprising that Paul didn't refer to the prayer in all his epistles. The history of reciting the prayer goes back to the early church practice of worship. The Lord's Prayer is taken for a perfect Creed on prayer. The primary purpose of a creed is not to guide only, but to first inform and then guide you. That is exactly the reason and the purpose of the prayer. It's a Christian Creed on prayer given by the Master Himself to inform us on what prayer is and to guide us over against a hypocritical and carnal form of prayer (Mt. 6:5-7). We recite the Lord's Prayer therefore, not as a special kind of prayer but as a Creed of prayer in order to keep to mind the most central truths of prayer and to help us watch against prejudice and vain repetition in prayer.

Second, the Lord's Prayer is not a master piece on the mechanics (principles) of prayer. There is no such thing in the whole Bible and, that is not an only justification that the "how-to" pray question is optional but that, a true prayer is not controlled by rules, chiefly because prayer is not a traditional action. To put it differently, prayer is not a human action but God. He is God the Holy Spirit who prays in us, and is not bound to rules. He is not limited. If you always pray the same way, the same words, take head! You aren't allowing God prays in you but doing your things by yourself. Rules on how to pray thrusts God out of the game and makes prayer mechanical. But prayer is God and of God. No man

THE LORD'S PRAYER

has known to master how to pray. In fact, a man who thinks to have mastered prayer has never prayed. The only perfect rule on how to pray is to pray.

Prayer is not eloquence nor a logical procession of words. Of course, there is a temptation of thinking that the disciples who ask: "teach us to pray" were carried away by Jesus' oration and logical projection of words. A true prayer, like the Gospel, is the "power of God" (Rom. 1:16). It doesn't come in words but in the power of the Holy Ghost. This form of prayer is characterized by fervency (James 5:16c-17b). Its virtue and power is not in rhetorical expression but the Holy Spirit praying in the good person. This is what Apostle Paul doubtlessly referring to when he says, "Pray in the Holy Ghost".

The disciples were being praying and, of course, they were prayer- warriors. But when they heard Jesus, their master praying, and sensed the power and saw the fervency in His prayer, they felt they had never prayed, and didn't know how to pray. They had no option but to ask Jesus "teach us to pray" (Lk. 11:1).

The truth is that, the more you pray, the less you think you haven't prayed and don't know how to pray. In other words, the more you pray, the more you want to learn to pray. If you rest complacent in your prayer life, you might not have being praying. On the contrary, if you are dissatisfied with your prayer life, you just feel you haven't prayed enough and don't know how to pray – rejoice! You are a prayerful man. Only be honest to ask with the disciples: "teach me to pray". The Lord's Prayer has the answer to your difficulty.

To pray is not to say a prayer or shout at God. We are sometimes tempted to think of those who say their great words, listen to its echo and become psychologically moved to consider themselves as prayer warriors. But that is not true. They are just shouting and saying a prayer. To pray is to pray in the Holy Ghost; to pray is to pray with fervency; to pray is to feel discourage the way you being praying and would like to learn to pray more. To pray, in short, is, like the disciples, to ask Jesus: "teach me to pray".

Prayer, we must admit, at this point, unlike the modern Christianity, is difficult. There is such emphasis on the simplicity of prayer these days than ever – that prayer is so simple and so easy – all you need to do is to carry your phone and dial J-E-S-U-S. There is 'no network busy', 'no switch off' or 'call again'. Everything about prayer is just formularized. But it's not true. In fact, the more you give formula to prayer and make it appears simple, the more it becomes difficult.

Lastly, the Lord's Prayer is not a master-piece on the meaning of prayer in a historical and theoretical context. Prayer is a present reality and action. We sometimes tend to look at prayer and understand it in a historical point of view, but not so here. Prayer is not history. Prayer is theology.

THE LORD'S PRAYER

Theology is God, and God does not change. "He is the same yesterday, today and forever". Amen.

The Lord's Prayer, in summary, is a Creed, a theology and worship. Most Christians have a superficial and one-sided view of prayer. For vast majority of Christians and scholars, prayer is a request, a communication of desires, needs, wants and emotions. But prayer is more than that. A true prayer is a true theology, a true worship.

A cursory reading of the Lord's Prayer reveals and substantiates the point. Vs. 9 of Mt. 6, talks about worship whereas vs.10-13, supplication. So you see, prayer is both worship and supplication. Our division of this subject is based on this fact.

We have written this booklet on the Lord's Prayer – having in mind – the same purpose for which it was ever taught. That is, to theologically inform and explain what prayer is and what to avoid in prayer. We therefore trust God to make you understand with us in this booklet what He has given us to pass across to you, and be of great importance to your life. Amen.

The Text

"But when ye pray, use not vain repetition, as the heathen do; for they think that they shall be heard for their much speaking. Be not ye therefore like unto them: for your father knoweth what things ye have need of, before ye ask him. After this manner therefore pray ye:

Our father which art in heaven, hallowed be thy name. Thy kingdom come. Thy will be done on earth, as it is in heaven. Give us this day our daily bread. And forgive us our debts, as we forgive our debtors. And lead us not into temptation, but deliver us from evil.

For if ye forgive men their trespasses, your heavenly Father will also forgive you. But if ye forgive not men their trespasses, neither will your Father forgive your trespasses. Mt. 6:7-15.

PART ONE:
WORSHIP

I

ADOPTION
Our father ...

Not so heard among so many great religions of the world to address God *Our Father* but in Christianity. Whether we take it for biological or rhetorical purpose, the phrase still stands for central biblical and theological truths. Any alternative translation or omission of the phrase is an injustice to the entire teaching of the Bible. The Good News and other versions of the Bible are surely mistaken to omit the pronoun, *our* from the phrase. They have done so because they stand oblivious to the great truths of the phrase. Let's look but few of these truths.

IMMANENCE OF GOD

Most people, even theological scholars have an abstract idea of God as a Being "up there" or "out there". God doesn't exist in reality but only in the mind. Closely to this, is the deistic view: God truly exists and creates the world but He has no dealing with it. He just sits up there like a wall clock to watch at the world. The world is on her own in all she does. Some religious groups, on the other hand, believe that God works in and through the world but has no direct and personal relationship and dealing with His creation. God is such a great and too holy Being that can't interact with the sinful world. He waits "up there" like a police man for people to sin to punish them. But the phrase discards all of these views as false.

God is a person, and He is personally related to His creation. He relates to and with Human beings in a parent-children relationship. He is to them a father in both creation and redemption.

The fatherhood of God reveals and points to His immeasurable and eternal love unto mankind (Gen. 1:26-31, John 3:16). God's love draws Him close to them to identify Himself with them as one of them in their make-up, thinking and emotion (personality). The Lord loves His creations – He cares and respects it. He preserves and provides for it. God is **our** father, Friend and Brother. The meaning of the church is Emmanuel, "God with us": God together with men and women. God is not separated from His creations. He is with them, He is among them, and He is one of them. We call Him *Our Father*.

But, that God is addressed Father doesn't mean God has a male gender. It is just a metaphor meant to express God's love which draws Him close to His creation. Meanwhile we should also watch against pantheistic spirit. That God is with and among His creation doesn't mean that God is everything and everything is God. Emanation is not accepted.

If God is our Father, then we are His children and, if children, then brothers and sisters. The pronoun *our,* was sensitively introduced to reject the idea and practice of individualism in both life and worship. Some people would like to address God, "My father" as if they were the only people with a heavenly descend. They think only of themselves and pray for themselves and their needs – that is all. But that is wrong. The <u>our</u> is to tell and keep reminding us that we are not standing in isolation to one another but in eternal unity. Christians all over the world are brothers and sisters irrespective of race, tribe, language, geography and culture. These are never barriers to our brotherhood and unity. God isn't a God of some particular individual groups or races in a particular space. He isn't interested in individualism. Whether in life or in prayer, the <u>our</u> is to remind us that Christians have one (same) descend, and therefore part of one another. A man who prays for himself and his needs – forgetting his fellow relatives in the Lord and body – is an individualist. God will not hear him. Christians everywhere in the world should live in love, care and service to one another. That is a true religion – to love your neighbors, fellow beings as yourself; to see them as brothers and sisters in the Lord without disparity in any external matter.

ADOPTION: A CRY FOR WORSHIP

We come now to our most significant part of our consideration. It's the question of a true prayer or worship.

What is a true worship? The term worship is so complicated to mean different things to different people at different time. For many scholars, worship refers to liturgical service. In contemporary Christianity, it means pulpit dictatorship, manipulation and interruption. A mechanical kind of worship characterizes by clapping of hands, shouting halleluiah, turning left and right to greet someone with smiling face, jumping up and down, sitting and standing up, or saying something after the preacher like:

Preacher: "Amen!"

Congregation: "Amen"!

Preacher: "Amen"!

Congregation: "Halleluiah!!"

Preacher: "The Lord is good"

Congregation: "All the time"

On a similar dimension, is the view that worship is an emotional disposition produce by some "prophetic utterances" and "mysterious songs". Immediately you begin to sing these songs, you will electrically be discharged to the spiritual mood and atmosphere where you become unconscious, then you begin to frown your face, wag your head, check your body, a kind of dizzying exercise, and sometimes fall on the ground and keep rolling like balloon till the Spirit is pleased to bring you back to your sense. The Spirit, according to this view, bypasses your reason and appeals to the emotion alone. Emotion is the regulatory principle and the defining feature in this kind of worship.

The last view is the celebrative view. Worship is celebration, celebration of birthday, prosperity, success in business, promotion in rank, a new car, new wife and husband, etc. which is characterized by eating and drinking, singing and dancing (music) as to oppose to suffering, failures and disappointments.

But as long as true worship is concerned in the biblical view, all these are important in their right places, yet doesn't stand central to the meaning of true worship.

A true worship, according to the Bible, is in Spirit and Truth (John 4:24). That is, on the opposite, a true worship isn't mechanical (dictatorship) nor psychological (emotionalism), but spiritual. This means that true worship isn't a human activity, action or response but of God the Spirit in human life and action.

The Holy Spirit is the Spirit of adoption (Sonship) (John 1:12, Gal. 3:26-29; 4:6-7). He bears witness with our spirits and we cry _Abba,_ Father (Roms. 8:14-17), of which I strongly believe and contend that Roms. 8: 14-17 is undeniably in line with the phrase _Our Father_ in the Lord's Prayer. No man can call God _our or My_ Father but the same

THE LORD'S PRAYER

who believes on His Son for salvation (John 1:12), of who is given the promise, the Holy Spirit of which, without Him, we are none of Christ (Roms. 8:9c). For by Him (the Spirit) we cry *Abba*, Father.

To worship in the Spirit and Truth therefore, is to cry *Abba*, Father, *Our Father*. To put it differently, true worship is a deep desire and yearning for God. It's having a sense of belonging and full assurance of faith in God. A true worship is setting of one's heart on things above (Col. 3:1-2); a true worship is meditating upon the words of God day and night and on whatever thing that is true, honest, just, pure, lovely, good, virtuous and praiseworthy (Psalm 1:3, Phil. 4:8); true worship is longing for conformity, where we groan, desiring to be clothed with our heavenly dwelling (2 Cor. 5:2); true worship is, in short, to cry *Abba*, Father, *Our Father*.

This worship is characterized by an inward joy of the Holy Ghost (Gal. 5:22) which is the strength of the believer, "Psalms, hymns, spiritual songs and making of melody in the heart to the Lord and giving of thanks" (Eph. 5:18-20), not by clapping and shouting at God. It is not accompanied by technical music nor necessarily by any demonstration; it's not limited to a worship Hall, neither to any sacraments, or rituals, not directed by any service leader, nor is it opposed to suffering, failure and disappointment. On the contrary, it desires to share in the crucifixion of Christ (Phil. 3:10-11) and, if so happens, it rejoices that it is counted worthy to suffer with Him (Acts 5:4,) knowing fully that, "tribulations worketh patience; and patience experience; and experience, hope and hope maketh not ashame" (Roms. 5:3-5). For "if so be that we suffer with Him, that we may also glorified together" (Roms. 8:17-18). A true worship is an unconditional celebration of life at the internal phase. It's joying in the Lord. This is our true glory.

This then is true worship which is true prayer – to yearn for God, *our father*.

II

ADORATION
… who art in heaven

TRANSCENDENCE OF GOD

While we affirm and emphasis that God is personal and personally relates to His creation as one of them in life and action, He is with them and to them, a Father who loves, cares and provides for their needs, Jesus doesn't let us think of God as an ordinary human being at all degrees and capacities of man. God is higher than human beings. *He is in heaven.* He can't be completely captured in human terms and treated in social context. Whether we understand the phrase as an abode of God up there or otherwise, it makes no difference. God is higher than men. What makes Him God is that He is not a man although He appeared in form of a man to identify with and atone for them.

We approach Him not as a Father, friend or brother now, but as a Creator, Redeemer and Lord of lords, a King. As a Creator, we marvel at the wonders of His wisdom, His inscrutable wisdom, His power and goodness in creation; as Redeemer and King, we submit in total obedience, bow to His throne and celebrate His victory over sin and death. We look at the beauty and mystery of the wind, we say, "wow! What a perfect designer could have designed the world?" No wonder, the psalmist would always worship the omniscience and omnipotence of God in creation (Psalm 19:1-).

This then is a true worship – to wonder at God, a transcendent God in existence, wisdom, power and everything. Being beyond our imagination and feeling, we stand in holy reverence and confess: "Lord, thou art God who hast made heaven, and earth, and the sea, and all that in them is" (Acts 4:24). You see, a true worship or adoration is an acknowledgement and confession of God as a Sovereign Being, freely independent of anything external to Him but Himself. Incomparable God, a Creator of everything (Isa. 40-49); true adoration is a total dependence on the power and wisdom of God (for provision, deliverance and protection (Psalm. 27, 46, Hab. 3:17-). Here is our glory and security. We boast of a God who knows all; a God whose power is unlimited, a God who is the creator of all things, a God who is not an idol, gods of the heathens, a God who is the Lord of lords, a God who can solve every serious problem in half second, a God who is an overcomer of sin and death. Man always believes, trusted, and takes security in "something" higher than himself. We pray to God who is in heaven, a God whose dwelling isn't with and among men but there above. We yearn for God who is perfectly wise, powerful and good, a God which, in Him is the fullness of joy and happiness, a God who liberates and gives freedom, a God, in short, *who art in heaven.*

Adoration therefore, isn't a rhetorical address of God as Creator, Lord, Redeemer, etc. but a sincere confession of the transcendental attributes of God and of depending on Him for living and success in life and work. It's to take comfort and security in this God who art in heaven. This is true worship, prayer.

III

HOLINESS
Hallow be thy name

We come now to the last element or component of a true worship (worship in spirit and truth), holiness. There is need to be careful at this point because of the difficulties surrounding our knowledge of God. To make ourselves explicit, we will quickly put our facts in propositional forms.

Let's begin by analyzing and defining the clause. Hallow means "sanctity", sacred. To hallow the name of the Lord means to "sanctify", "make sacred or holy", "set apart" His name. His name there refers to the whole of His personality, His very essence. The clause, you notice, is translated in verb, action form – meaning that holiness is an action. In other words, worship as a verb is holiness.

The reason and purpose of making the name of the Lord holy is because God Himself is holy (Lev. 19, 1 Pet. 1:15-16). His holiness is strongly and immediately opposed to evil and every evil thought and action in a judgmental order (the wrath of God). This leads us to the incurable tension between God's love, Fatherhood (immanence) and His wrath, a holy indignation.

Modern Christianity are completely digested and assimilated in the idea of God's love only to think of a wrathful God as different or another God which isn't the other. God is love, how can He be an angry God, a "consuming fire" even to punish His disobedient creatures to Hell? For to love, is to will the good of someone; to be willing to forgive your enemies. If God will not forgive but to condemn to hell, is He then a good God? Is He the God whom we believe? Is He the God depicted in the Gospels, John 3:16 in particular? Have we not got to believe a different God? Should we not, like the Gnostics and Marcionists take this God for the Old Testament God, full of wrath and anger, unwilling to forgive, ever ready to punish sinners, an evil God, a God, unlike the New Testament God, is strict in His dealing with wrongdoers?

Whatever we think and say of God in relation to His love and holiness is directly owing to our ignorance. That God is love doesn't mean He doesn't punish. Then, that is a false love. A love that isn't displeased with evil life isn't a true love (1 Cor. 13:4-7). And that men, sinful men and women are punished to hell isn't God's decision but of them. God must be justified, man condemned. Man is given a freewill to choose and decide what is good and , he is given condition to salvation but he prefers his own way and so is condemned (John 3: 18-19). God is absolutely just in His doings.

We have seen that the chief reason and purpose for holiness and holy life isn't that we should be good people in and to ourselves but because God is holy, so ought we, be holy who call upon His name. This explains the need and necessity of holiness in our life and actions. The argument is simple. If we claim to believe in this God who is our Father, and who art in heaven, a God whose name is holy, a God who is "light and in Him is no darkness at all" (1 John 1:5), if truly He is our Father, and share life with Him (communion and fellowship) in sincerity, then is nothing of the highest priority than a quest for holiness and righteousness (2 Tim. 2:22). "For if we say that we have fellowship with Him, and walk in darkness, we lie, and do not the truth. But if we walk in the light, as He is in the light, we have fellowship with one another, and the blood of Jesus Christ cleanseth us from all sin" (1 John 1:6-7). "For without holiness no one can see the Lord" (Hebrew 12:14). "Blessed are pure in heart for they shall see God" (Mt. 5:7).

The question is: how do we preserve and make known the holiness of the Lord? In other words, how can we hallow, make holy the name of the Lord? By fearing His name. To fear God is to hate evil (Prov. 8:13). Should you not fear this God who is far beyond the grasp of men, this God who is the creator of heaven and earth by living a holy life unto His name?

THE LORD'S PRAYER

To hallow the name of the Lord, I repeat is to hate evil and every appearance of it at all times in every place; to hallow the name of the Lord isn't to shout in words of praise to His name but to live a life of holiness to this name. A true worship is true holiness. If you profess religion or faith in God, even the true God, but live a different life, a life not in conformity to your faith, you deceive yourself; if you claim to be a prayer man, a worshiper of God in Spirit and truth but, go about chasing girls on the street, lying, cheating, listening to sexy music, watching blue films and pornographies, reading of romantic novels, you are a false worshiper.

To say that God is holy is simple but not enough, until you can live out the holiness. To sing:

Higher – 2x

Jesus higher

I will lift

My Jesus higher

Every day

Only to do the opposite is easy but not enough until you can lift Him up by your life, not by mere words in singing. "Let every man who is named the name of Christ depart from iniquity" (2 Tim. 2:19). "I beseech you therefore, brethren, by the mercies of God, that ye present your bodies as a living sacrifices, holy acceptable unto God, which is your reasonable service…" (Rom. 12:1-2, 1 Cor. 6:19-20, 2 Cor. 6:14-18). This is true worship – to "present yourself as a living sacrifices, holy and acceptable unto God", to come out of the world, to separate yourself.

PART TWO:

SUPPLICATION

I

REVIVAL

Thy kingdom come. Thy will be done on earth as it is in heaven

Having seen what prayer is — that prayer is worship and in return, worship is, in a summary, adoption, adoration and holiness, we turn now to the section that deals with the second meaning of prayer, supplication. The main reason and purpose of the Lord's Prayer, I emphasis, is to teach us what prayer is and to correct our common errors in prayer.

The common error, in our daily prayer, and, of course with a parlous result is subjectivism, something Jesus calls vain repetition (Mt. 6:7-8). Some people understand the phrase as to mean mere repetition of words. But if it were so, we are all guilty of that error. Vs. 8 doesn't consent with this interpretation. As long as vss. 7-8 is concerned, this is wrong judgment. Every action, no matter how good it is, doesn't stand on its own and shouldn't be taken on its own.

THE LORD'S PRAYER

Every action or expression must be seen, taken and judged in relation to the motive of doing or saying it. What makes praying on the street or synagogue wrong, isn't praying on the street, but the motive for praying on the street. Accordingly, what makes our prayer vain repetition isn't mere repetition of words, but the motive we have in repeating ourselves. If this isn't true, then we may as well judge the expression, "holy, holy, holy, is the Lord God" as vain repetition. David, of course, should be guilty of vain repetition. For nothing is apparently notice in the prayers of David than constant recurring words, phrases and clauses.

However, on the opposite, the vain repetitions refer to subjectivism. Repetition in words or actions points to area of concern. Vain repetition therefore, is a concern for something which has a secondary value in life. On the other way round, it is a concern, a putting first materialism instead of God's kingdom and its righteousness (Mt. 6:33). Man is concern for himself and his needs and so, he begins his requests with and for himself and his needs. What matters is materialism, not salvation. Materialism is the meaning of life. But Jesus seriously warns us against this error insomuch that He devotes vs. 19-34-proving by claims of fact and of reason (logic) – why we shouldn't fall into this error and let our hearts trouble for materialism. It doesn't affect anything and mark the difference from the pagans in that regard. What we should do and always do is to "put first the kingdom of God and its righteousness, and all these things shall be added unto us. We should begin our request with God and His needs before ourselves. God first, man second. There is no subjectivism in prayer. Jesus condemns it.

Now that which is pertained to God and His will of which, we are to love most, concern and pray for, that is, His kingdom and its righteousness — is what I call Revival, the "Thou -petitions" as some would prefer it. Revival therefore, is a concern, a putting first the kingdom of God and it's righteousness; it's a desire for the salvation of men and women and of reawakening and enlivening of a spiritually dead and sleeping souls to a state of religious zeal and commitment; it's a concern for the growth and expansion of God's kingdom and of doing His will on earth; it's to refuse to keep quite or silence and to give God rest until He makes this world His kingdom and causes His will to be done in it (Isa. 62:1-7); it's to labour fervently in prayers for the church of God to be established in doing God's will (Col. 4:12); in short, it's to say, "Let thy kingdom come. Thy will be done on earth as it is in heaven".

There was a time in church history where men and women couldn't rest, sleep, eat, walked naked, persecuted but never troubled. That was the kingdom of God and its righteousness. They held discussions on how to promote it; organized prayer meetings and preached in respect to it. The result was Revival (evangelical heritage). But alas! What an opposite today! Our request is characterized by materialism and denominationalism. We are concerned only with ourselves and our particular denominations, and pray only for its traditions and members. One who isn't identified with a certain denomination isn't a Christian, but an enemy. We shouldn't pray for his salvation but destruction. Christianity is at stake because of materialism and denominationalism. Men and women have refused to be evangelical. To be evangelical, is to be a revivalist. That is, to put first the kingdom of God and its righteousness. I think, there is an urgent need for us evangelicals to stand on our feet to save and strengthen that which is left.

If we yearn for God who art in heaven, and whose name is holy and should be hallowed, but struggle not to help promote the growth and expansion of His kingdom, we are not praying and don't know how to pray. We must ask: "teach us to pray". To pray is to say, "Let thy kingdom come. Thy will be done on earth as it's in heaven". He who prays this way is ready to sacrifice himself, his time and resources for the growth and expansion of God's kingdom. True worship isn't about yearning for God – characterize by joy, singing and praising God in the heart only, but also about profession and proclamation.

The next perplexing question is to whether this request is of a present or eschatological value. Is this prayer concerned with the second advent of Christ as a King when He shall bring an end to evil and establish a perfect kingdom on earth, or is it concerned with the apparent growth and expansion of His kingdom as in the salvation of men and women and, of doing His will here on earth as still in the flesh?

Another difficulty is that: is the expression, "let thy kingdom come" referring to the advent of the Holy Spirit or Christ Himself? For some, the former. I could remember very well one of my lecturers from Liberty Bible College and Seminary (LBCS) contending that there is no meaning to praying that "let thy kingdom come" because the kingdom had already come. The Holy Spirit is the kingdom, and He had come on the Pentecost Day. His argument is that Jesus, at the time when He taught His disciples this prayer, the Holy Spirit hadn't come because He (Jesus) hadn't yet ascended into heaven. So by this request He was asking His disciples to pray for the coming of the Holy Ghost which finally came on the Pentecost Day. And now that the Holy Spirit which is the Kingdom we should pray for is come, what is the meaning of praying for the kingdom to come again? What kingdom do we expect more? The Holy Ghost is the kingdom and is come. That is all. "The kingdom of God", he said, "Is in righteousness, peace and joy in the Holy Ghost" (Roms. 14:17). We possess and carry the Holy Ghost in and with us. That is the kingdom.

But this is directly in travesty to the teaching of the Bible concerning the God-head, Trinity. There is never a kingdom without a king, and nowhere in the Bible is the Holy Ghost represented as a King but Christ. We can't expect the kingdom (government) without the king. Christ is the King. To pray for the coming of the kingdom is to pray for the coming of Christ, even the second coming.

THE LORD'S PRAYER

Do we now say the prayer is eschatological? Yes. But the question is: how can Christ come when men and women haven't heard the Gospel, and are dying in their sins? How can He come when we haven't preached the gospel unto the entire world? (Mt. 24:14; Acts 1:6-8). There is no way for and to the kingdom of glory but first the kingdom of grace. Men shall be saved first. Then shall He come. Therefore, the quest stands for both present and future value. We should pray for the salvation of men and for the second coming of Christ to judge and reign forever.

III

SURVIVAL
Give us this day, our daily bread

Our God isn't an ego-centric God. He cares also for our needs. His warning is that we shouldn't crave after materialism but the kingdom of God and its righteousness. Materialism isn't the meaning of life. Materialism is destructive. It can turn you from God (Prov. 5:7). Materialism, in short, is vanity (Eccl. 1:1). After all, nobody came with wealth neither shall we leave away with something in our hands. As we came, so shall we return (Job 1:21, Eccls. 5:9-10, 14; 1 Tim. 6:7). The first thing first isn't materialism but life. Life is better than food and raiment (vs. 25c of Mt 6).

God knows and cares for our needs. He provides even for the birds of the air that are nothing to Him compare to man who was made in His image, and for man's sake, He suffered and died a shameful death on the cross. Shall He not do much more unto us than the birds of the air that exist today and vanish tomorrow? "Are we not much better than they?" what are we different for, from the pagans who seek after the same thing? If we gain the whole world but loose our souls, what does it profit us? "O ye of little faith!" Learn your lesson.

The cheap thing God can ever give us is money. For if He had given us life eternal which caused Him His life, what more of material things that are perishable? (John 6:25-27). The kingdom of God and its righteousness which is to us life eternal is the best and the first. Food and raiment are secondary needs. God knows about it, He will provide it to us.

But the common objection is, if God knows our needs why should we ask Him for it before He provides to us? For most persons, this isn't fair. But that is rebellion.

That we ask God for our needs is an acknowledgment and confession that God is our provider, not ourselves. To put it differently, it's an act of faith. Faith is waiting on God for provision and protection. There is no meaning and need for thanksgiving if we don't believe God our provider. We give thanks in appreciation of His benevolent deeds. Acknowledging that all things we have are given us by God. Man isn't the sustainer of himself.

Praying to God for our needs is also a request for permission from God to legally use His abundant blessings. A man who doesn't ask God for permission to use His gifts is a great thief. For if God is the giver of everything, we must ask Him for permission as well as for direction on how to use His blessings. What is wrong with stealing is that the thief doesn't ask for permission. He takes it without the knowledge of the owner and so, refuses to give thanks to him. That is the argument. We are thieves and ungrateful whatsoever, as long as we refuse to ask God for provision of our needs and permission to use them and by that, we claim self-dependence.

The idea of bread in the petition isn't limited to food and raiment only, but to as many good things as necessary for good health and holy living. It includes education, good house, new brand cars, possibly jeeps, airplanes, good phones etc. we should ask for all these things but be careful to employ them to the right end. The way we obtain and use wealth matters a lot. It can work for our good or destruction.

We are wisely counseled to ask for today's needs, the present needs only. Don't ask for something to keep in store only to be making your boast. God will not give you. Ask for what is of greatly needful to you at the moment. God's provision is based on the necessary needs of the time. If I have no genuine reason or need for asking for wealth, God will not give. I should ask to solve my needs not to compete with others. God looks at your motive and your present need of the time to answer your request. Pray for things that are presently needed and necessary for your living in faith and love.

IV

CONFESSION
...forgive us our debts, as we forgive our debtors

There are two great theological temptations liable to every Christian and theologian. The first is perfectionism, the second antinomianism. There are some Christians of a notion and practice that if you become a Christian, you become an angel. There is no more sin and sinning again. Or that you at least, struggle to be perfect while in this life. Jesus said, according to this group, "Be ye therefore perfect, even as your Father which is in heaven perfect" (Mt. 5:48, 1 Pet. 1:15-16). Christianity is therefore, a perfect religion of perfect persons that never in a single moment make the least mistake. That is the impression that is left on the average people in Christian community and the wider society. The pagans live in constant inspection to see how these "special angels" of humankind live their lives. Shamefully enough, they look at us stumbling; they look at us going back to the world and conforming to her standards of living, and so become astonish and mock at us. Looking at how we treat backsliders and those who fall into temptation in the Christendom, some nominal members of the faith said, "they will not answer the call to repentance until the time they prepare their minds never to sin again in their life-time – for they fear they will do the same mistake they saw others doing".

The perfectionist objection is, since we can attain perfection as the Buddhist can attain <u>Nirvana,</u> state of perfect life, why need we pray for forgiveness? Are we still sinful? Have we not attained the state of sinlessness? A man ever asked me to pray, after the prayer he asked me, "What more sin did I get to confess? Hadn't God forgiven our sins once and for all the day we repent? What is He to forgive me again?" His argument is theologically sound. But it's a half way, an uncompleted theology of sin and forgiveness. Sanctification isn't an automatic game but a process. The doctrine of eschatology justifies it. The Christian man is still a man. He is in the flesh and blood. He is weak and can sin although he doesn't sin.

I suppose John had these people in mind when he wrote his first epistle. The purpose of the epistle was to warn against such error. We shouldn't forget that the epistle was written to believers like us, people who confess Christ for Saviour and Lord. But then, they seemed to be carried away by their theological logic of 'if this… then… that'. John in vs. 8-10 condemns perfectionism forever. "If we say that we have no sin', in other words, if we claim perfection, 'we

THE LORD'S PRAYER

deceive ourselves, and the truth isn't in us" (vs. 8. Rather, on the contrary, 'if we confess our sins", in other way round, if we say, "forgive us our debts, as we forgive our debtors", "God is faithful and just to forgive us our sins and cleanse us from all unrighteousness (vs. 9). If on the other hand, we deny the reality of the fall, then we make God a liar and His word isn't in us (vs. 10).

To end the matter in a single statement, sanctification is a process. It begins with and from regeneration, but continues till the day of redemption (rapture) (Eph. 4:30). There is no perfectionism in Christianity.

The antinomians on the other hand emphasis the grace of God at the expense of the law. Man is saved by grace, not by the deeds of the law. The law therefore, is abrogated and there is no need and value to keeping the law. Salvation by grace is effectual. Whether you deliberately sin or not, you still make heaven. You are saved and saved forever (predestination). Man is therefore, free in and to everything. He isn't bound to and by the law.

A new version of this group today is dispensationalism. We, unlike the Jews are in the dispensation of grace and therefore, free from the law. It doesn't matter how we live our lives. We can sin and continue in sinning, there is an abundant grace for us. God is loving, gracious and merciful - ever ready to forgive our sins. All we need to do is to confess our sins, and go back to sinning again. That is the kind of life we should live.

But alas, what an inconceivable idea and practice! There is no error the Bible relentlessly condemns and seriously warns against than this. "God is light, and in Him is no darkness at all. If we say that we have fellowship with Him, and walk in darkness, we lie, and do not know the truth" (1 John 1:5c-6) "Do we continue in sin that grace may abound?" "put not your trust in the deceitful words: "This is the temple of the Lord", only if you thoroughly reform your ways and your deeds: if each of you deals justly with his neighbor; if you no longer oppress the resident alien, the orphan, and the widow; if you no longer shed innocent blood in this place, or follow strange gods to your own harm, will I remain with you in this place, in the land which I gave your fathers long ago and forever. Are you to steal and murder, commit adultery and perjury, burn incense to Baal, go after strange gods that you know not, and yet come to stand before me in this house which bears my name, and say: "we are safe; we can commit all these abominations again"? Has this house which bears my name become in your eyes a den of thieves? I too see what is being done, says the Lord" (Jer. 7:4-7, 9-11).

The point is, in short, to take the law and holiness for flippancy and jocularity, is enough proof that you are not a Christian. Grace that doesn't humble is no true grace. Away with your stubborn grace.

Another important truth about this particular request is that, forgiveness is both vertical and horizontal practice, and as a matter of fact, the vertical seems to rest on the horizontal

THE LORD'S PRAYER

(Mt. 6:14. We all know that Jesus is here talking to His disciples, people who believed in Jesus and had their sins forgiven. They had tasted of the joy of forgiveness. If this same people, wretched and miserable, "who weren't people, but now people, who haven't obtain mercy, who have tasted of the grace of God and experience the joy of forgiveness", will refuse to forgive those who wrong them, God will not forgive them (Mt. 18:21-35). A Christian who asks God for forgiveness of his sins must be sure that he has forgiven them who sinned against him, and always willing and ready to forgive them, or otherwise, he deceives himself.

Forgiveness is an absolute necessary for peace-keeping (fellowship) and continuity of life. "If possible, live at peace with everyone". There is no peace without forgiveness, whatsoever. Peace is the resultant effect of forgiveness. A man who doesn't forgive is always at war, struggling, wrestling in his heart. "There is no peace for the wicked, says my God". Forgive, and be forgiven; forgive, and have peace of mind.

V

DELIVERANCE

And lead us not into temptation, but deliver us from evil

The best way to proceed with this consideration is to first define our terms. The word temptation is ambiguous. It has double phase. It refers first, to persecution and second, to enticement. We can quickly notice it in the epistles of James and Peter and also in the Gospel of Matthew. James used the word in 1.2-3 to refer to persecution. "My brethren, count it all joy when ye fall into divers *temptations*; knowing this, that the trying of your faith worketh patience" (1Pet. 1:6-7) also, "wherein ye greatly rejoice, though now for a season, if need be, ye are in heaviness through manifold *temptations*: that the trial of your faith, being much more precious than of gold that perisheth, though it be tried with fire, might be found unto praise and honor and glory at the appearing of Jesus Christ"'. Vs. 13-14 of James chapter 1 has something different but similar in mind from temptation as persecution. Here he talks about temptation as enticement or deception. "Let no

THE LORD'S PRAYER

man say when he is tempted, I am tempted of God for God cannot be tempted with, neither tempteth He any man; but every man is tempted, when he is drawn away of his own lust, and enticed' (See also Mt. 4).

Nevertheless, the term stands for the general word *test*. "A test of our faith". Our faith is tested by both *persecution* and *enticement* to evil, worldliness. Daniel's faith was tested by fire (persecution); Jesus faith was tested by deception and enticement to worldliness (Dan. 3 & Mt. 4 respectively). A true faith, according to the Bible, is that which when it's tested by persecution, doesn't relinquish, and when it's tested by worldliness doesn't succumb to it.

That then is the Biblical sense of the term. But there is more to it by extension. The word goes far to include every misfortune and natural disaster such as sickness or ill-health, demon possessed, earthquake etc. Jesus taught His disciples to humbly ask God for deliverance. That is, in other way round, temptation is inevitable. It must always come and be there to befall us. We aren't asked to pray against it as to eliminate it forever in the world but to be delivered from it. A prayer therefore, that is characterized by such expression as, "I cast you into the lake of fire, in the name of Jesus", "let my enemies perish, in the name of Jesus', "Holy Ghost!!!... Fire!!!..., is nothing but simple ignorance. We are to cast out demons but not to hell, to pray for the salvation of our enemies, not for their destruction. Condemnation to death or hell isn't for us but God. Resist no evil (Mt. 5:3a).

Note, God isn't and never to be blamed, especially for the temptation of worldliness (James 1:13-14). We are often time too soon to blame God for every bad-luck. "He knows everything, He knows about this, even before it happens. Why did He not stop it?" But let it be known to us once and for all that, the original cause of every temptation in the world is sin, man's disobedience, not God. If we propend to worldliness and fall into it, it's our lust that causes us, not God (James 1:14). If we are persecuted, it's the consequences of our sin not God. "I will put enmity between you and the woman and between your offspring and hers; he will strike your head, while you strike at his heel" (Gen. 3:15). God is just, man is his trouble.

Another crucial fact is that, praying for deliverance goes with watchfulness. In fact, generally, prayer (as supplication) without action is dead. To pray, is to watch and to watch, is to pray. If I pray for deliverance from ill-health, but fail to keep hygienic rules and practice, I refuse to see the doctor, I refuse to take the prescribed drugs, what good is my prayer for?; if I pray for deliverance from worldliness, but fail to flee away at the appearance of evil, fail to be self-control, fail to put on the whole armour of God, what good is my prayer?; if I pray for peace, but fail to work at making and building peace, fail to forgive my offenders, fail to forgive my enemies, what is the prayer for?; if I pray for wealth, but refuse to farm, refuse to work, what good is the prayer; if I pray for knowledge, but refuse to read, refuse to go to school, to what end is the prayer? Let's not deceive ourselves. We should work our request out. Every prophecy is fulfilled under two conditions: God's responsibility and man's. So is prayer. You should be watchful as we pray for deliverance or otherwise, we deceive ourselves.

Notes

Ayo, Nicholas. *The Lord's Prayer*. London: University of Notre Dame Press, 1992.

Carson, D.A, *Worship*, Grand Rapids Michigan; Zondervan, 2007.

Carson, D.A. *Worship, Adoration Action*. Grand Rapids Michigan Baker Book House, 1993.

DYK, Van Leanne. *A more profound Alleluia*. Grand Rapids, Michigan: William, B. Eerdmans publishing company, 2005.

Earl, C. Davis. *Forever Amen*. Nashville, Tennessee; Boardman press. 1982

Evely, Louis. *Teach Us How to Pray* (New York: Paulest Press, 1967).

Farhadian, E. Charles, *Christian Worship Worldwide*, Grand Rapids, Michigan; William .B. Eerdmans publishing company, 2007.

Helmut, Thuelicke. *Our Heavenly Father*, New York; Harper & Row, publishers, 1960.

Hurtado, W. Larry. At the Origin or Christian Worship. Grand Rapids, Michigan: William .B. Eerdmans publishing company, 1999.

Jeremias, Joachuru. *The Prayers of Jesus*. SCM press LTD 1967

Keith, Pecklers F. *Worship*, London; continuum, 2003.

McGrath, E. Alister. *Christian Theology*. Victoria: Blackwell publishing 2001.

Micheal, Green. *Jesus – Man of Prayer*. London; Hodder and sloughton, 1987.

Philip, Keller W. *A Lay Man looks At the Lord's Prayer*, Minneapolis, Minnesota; worldwide publications, 1976.

R.J, Gore. Covenantal Worship. New Jersey; P & R publishing, 2002.

Raymond, L. Robert. *A New Systematic Theology of the Christian Faith*, Nashville: Thomas Nelson publishers, 1998.

Robert, Webber E. *Worship is a Verb*. Peabody, Massachusetts, 2004.

Thomas, Schattauer H. Worship in an Age of Mission. Minneapolis: Fortress, 1999.

Tracy, Joseph. *The Great Awakening*. Britain: Banner of Truth Trust, 1997.

Watson, Thomas. *The Lord's Prayer,* London; Banner of Truth Trust, 1989.

Webber, E. Robur. *Worship Old and New*. Grand Rapids, Michigan; Zondervan, 1994.

White, F. James. *Protestant Worship*. Counsville, Kentucky, Westminster, 1989.

Wiersbe, W. Warren. *Real Worship*. Grand Rapids, Michigan; Baker Books, 2000.

Zrickson, J. Millard. *Christian Theology*. Grand Rapids, Michigan; Baker book House, 1985.

www.ingramcontent.com/pod-product-compliance
Lightning Source LLC
Chambersburg PA
CBHW050046080526
44586CB00014B/1483